Published by Intuitive Arts Media LLC

IntuitiveArtsMedia.com

Copyright © Isabeau Maxwell 2021

All rights reserved. No parts of this publication may be reproduced or transmitted in whole or in part, in any form or by any means, electronic or mechanical, including photocopying, recording, or by any information storage and retrieval system, without permission in writing from Intuitive Arts Media.

ISBN: 978-1-7351911-7-1 (paperback)

Disclaimer:

This workbook is designed to provide information and motivation to our readers. It is understood that the publisher is not engaged to render any type of psychological, legal, or any other kind of professional advice. The content is the sole expression and opinion of the author and not necessarily that of the publisher. No warranties or guarantees are expressed or implied by the publisher's choice to include any content in this volume. Neither the publisher nor the individual author shall be liable for any physical, psychological, emotional, financial, or commercial damages, including but not limited to special, incidental, consequential, or other damages. Our views and rights are the same: You are responsible for your own choices, actions, and results.

Although the author and publisher have made every effort to ensure that the information in this book was correct at press time, the author and publisher do not assume and hereby disclaim any liability to any party for loss, damage, or disruption caused by errors or omissions, whether such errors or omissions result from negligence, accident, or any other cause.

This workbook belongs to:

_____

Table of Contents

ii	How to Use This Workbook
1	Session One: Reclaiming Your Focus
27	Session Two: Core Vs. Culture
47	Session Three: Negativity and Perspective
69	Session Four: Organization
95	Session Five: Guides and Manifesting
105	Session Six: How Everything Works
113	Session Seven: The Experiments
119	What's Next?
120	About the Author
	Book Recommendations

How to Use this Wookbook

This journal belongs to you, just you. This is where you will record and witness your journey unfold. Your SAGE Method journal is your safe place to write down your thoughts, experiences, and ideas. As you step into this transformation, this will be your spot to check in, check off tasks, and keep your spiritual path in front of you. Make sure to connect with your journal daily while you are in the course to support the growth of your new and exciting spiritual practices.

This is your time! This is where you step into your greatness and create the life you want. Stick with the course through all the worksheets and tasks. The more you put into this SAGE Method formula, the more you will gain from it. Don't hesitate or be shy. Dive in!

Session 1

Reclaiming Your Focus

Let's dive in! This first session we will evaluate how we position ourselves energetically and spiritually. Accessing strong intuition happens when we are positioned correctly in our lives and solidly on our spiritual path. To achieve this, we need to gain awareness of where we are right now, readjust where needed, and step into the flow. With some valuable spiritual practices under our belt this week, we are on our way!

Topics Include:
Intuitive Abilities
Belief and Faith
Responses and Reactions
Energetic and Spiritual Protection

Worksheets

The Ten Keystones of Spiritual Ethics
Examples of Intuitive Abilities
The Special Factor
Energetic and Spiritual Protection (GCP)
Respond vs. React
The Brick Wall
No Doubt Notebook
Five-Minute Faith Practice
Nightly Evaluations
Self-Evaluation

Homework Checklist

- [ ] The Special Factor
- [ ] Respond vs. React
- [ ] The Brick Wall
- [ ] Self-Evaluation

Daily To-Do's for Students

Nightly Evaluations
- [ ] - [ ] - [ ] - [ ] - [ ] - [ ] - [ ]

GCP
- [ ] - [ ] - [ ] - [ ] - [ ] - [ ] - [ ]

No Doubt Notebook
- [ ] - [ ] - [ ] - [ ] - [ ] - [ ] - [ ]

Five-Minute Faith Practice
- [ ] - [ ] - [ ] - [ ] - [ ] - [ ] - [ ]

The 10 Keystones of Spiritual Ethics

Always Ask Permission

Respect the receiver by asking permission before passing along intuitive information or sending healing energy. A person's permission is key to transferring information or energy.

Never Assume You Can Help

You are simply a hollow bone. How the intuitive information or healing energy is received is up to the receiver and their higher powers.

You Are Just The Messenger

Intuitive information comes from guides, spirits and higher powers. They provide the information and you simply deliver it. Your opinion is not a factor.

Respect Personal Belongings

Always ask permission before holding someone's personal belongings. When someone gives you an object to hold, honor it. It is special to them and should be to you as well.

Never Give Medical Advice

Unless you are a medical professional, it is not legal for you to give medical advice. When you receive intuitive information of a medical nature, always refer the person to a medical professional.

Always Be Grateful

A position of gratitude is the best position for intuition and healing energy. It is in a state of gratitude we are given the ability to do our work.

Balance Your Human and Spiritual Paths

Losing yourself to your human path disconnects you from your higher self. Losing yourself to your spiritual path disconnects you from your existence. Both extremes are empty of benefits.

Respect All Paths

No one path is the right path. Everyone's journey is sacred. Respect each person's journey as if it was your own.

Always Be Learning

When learning stops, so does growth. An active mind and a curious mind is open to expansion.

Always Be Honest

To speak a lie is to clutter yourself and it serves no one.

Examples of Intuitive Abilities

Everyone's intuition is unique! No two people are the same. However, culture has provided us with names of different abilities in hopes to categorize them. While this list is a sample of some of the more well known abilities, it is in no way a complete or fully descriptive list of intuitive possibilities. Do not let this list limit you! Read it as a point of interest, not as a boundary.

The main categories of abilities are described as **clairs**:

Clairvoyance	clear seeing, vision
Clairaudience	clear hearing with inner or outer ears
Clairsentience	messages through physical feeling
Clairalience	messages through smell
Claircognizance	messages through knowing
Clairgustance	messages through tasting

Other abilities include:

Animal Communication - The ability to intuitively communicate with creatures/animals

Astral Projection - The ability to leave one's body and travel in spirit to another location

Aura Reading - The ability to see energy fields that emanate from living beings

Automatic Writing - Writing through the subconscious mind without conscious thought, or through the guidance of an outside intelligence

Channeling - Associated with mediums, this is the ability to act as a channel or vessel for an outside intelligence, there are many definitions of channeling

Divination - A broad term that includes fortune telling, precognition, prophesy, and other methods used in an effort to predict the future

Empathy - The ability to sense the needs, drives and emotions of another

Levitation - The ability to cause one's body to hover off the ground or fly

Precognition - Simply, "knowing the future"

Psychometry - Also known as "object reading," psychometry enables a person to pick up on psychic impressions (vibrations) left on an object by someone connected with it

Pyrokinesis - The ability to start fires with one's mind

Telekinesis - Also known as psychokinesis, the ability to move objects with one's mind

Telepathy - The ability to communicate mind-to-mind with another

Scrying - a visual method of precognition

Remote Viewing - the ability to see something that is not within physical sight

The Special Factor

List three abilities, not related to intuition, that make you special or unique.
_____
_____
_____

List three personal qualities, not related to intuition, that make you helpful or kind.
_____
_____
_____

List three life accomplishments, not related to intuition, that make you proud.
_____
_____
_____

Energetic & Spiritual Protection

An effective tool to balance your spiritual world

The spiritual world affects us daily in positive, beautiful ways, and sometimes in chaotic, uncomfortable ways. Spiritually clearing, grounding, and protecting is a statement of reclaiming your personal spiritual space and bringing you closer to your life path. This practice has proven to be priceless to those who use it.

This protection practice filters out unnecessary negativity and unnecessary uncomfortable spiritual encounters. It is protective but will not isolate you or shut you down. In fact, this process has been known to bring more positivity and amazing connections into people's lives. It will speed your growth and ease the stress involved with personal and spiritual interaction.

This is a practice of intention. The combination of creating visuals in your mind and using strong intention and belief creates effective results. At first, this practice may take some time. With repetitive use, it takes less than ten seconds to do.

When you begin this practice, do it at least twice a day and at any point in which you feel uncomfortable. If after doing the practice, a negative situation still affects you, then that particular situation is important to your path and should be dealt with as needed. We should always be working to establish healthy personal boundaries in life. More likely than not, you will find a quick ground-clear-protect (GCP) will alleviate emotional distress within you and allow you to separate yourself from the drama that is not yours.

For energy workers, this process will assist you in becoming more present in your work. More importantly, it will allow you to release what is not yours to carry, the negative energy you may have encountered when working with a client.

In addition to doing this practice for your own personal energetic space, this is a process you can also apply to your home, children, and loved ones. Always ask someone's permission before doing it, and set the intention of doing it for their highest good.

Be creative with your visuals. Make this practice personal by using elements and images important to you. This will heighten your intent and empower the practice. If you struggle with visualization, simply say the words out loud and trust that your voice speaks for your soul.

Directions for GCP

Remember, Intent is Everything!

Step 1. Ground Yourself

Begin by grounding yourself. Ask Mother Earth to anchor you, to hold you safely and securely. For example, imagine your legs sinking into the ground, or tree roots coming out of your bare feet, branching into the earth. When we ground, we are asking to be held and supported as we go higher spiritually. Just like a tree, the deeper it is rooted, the taller it can climb. The support of the earth will center you and give you the opportunity to go safely go spiritually higher.

Step 2. Clear Yourself

In your mind, use the image of wind, water, air, or any other element to clear yourself of negative energy, feelings or ailments. Be creative and use what resonates with you. Imagine water pouring through you, washing away negativity. Or, visualize wind blowing through your body releasing darkness. With the element of your choice, see the negative energy leaving your body. Witness the black clouds or sludge being cleared out of your personal space. Once the negative energy is outside of your space, ask for it to be transformed into positive energy so as to not affect other people negatively.

Step 3. Protect Yourself

Next, build an energetic "shell" to protect the balance you have just created. You can start with a bubble unless something else resonates with you more strongly. Make sure your protection is impenetrable; allow the bubble walls to be thick if needed. Have confidence that in this space you are safe.

Step 4. Intention Speech

Let your guides and loved ones on the otherside know the purpose of your protection. Speak your statement out loud or in your mind. A good statement might sound like... "May all negative energy bounce off me and be sent back to spirit, and to sender, with love. Please allow only my highest good to come through." By asking for the negative energy to be sent back with love, you are actively walking through this world making it a better place!

Respond vs. React

Record three situations where you were given the choice to respond or react, and answer the questions that follow.

Situation No. 1
_____

Did you respond or react?
_____

If you reacted, how did the energy affect you during and after the situation?
_____

If you responded, what benefit did you gain from the situation?
_____

Situation No. 2
_____

Did you respond or react?
_____

If you reacted, how did the energy affect you during and after the situation?
_____

If you responded, what benefit did you gain from the situation?
_____

Situation No. 3
_____

Did you respond or react?
_____

If you reacted, how did the energy affect you during and after the situation?
_____

If you responded, what benefit did you gain from the situation?
_____

The Brick Wall

List one problem in your life that is not resolving itself as fast as you would like it to. This could be a problem in a relationship, a problem with money, your career, your personal self, etc.

_____
_____

What role do you play in this situation continuing and not resolving?

_____
_____

What are you doing that is not working that you need to do less of?

_____
_____

What are you currently doing that is working that you could do more of?

_____
_____

What are you not doing that you could try on to see if it works?

_____
_____

What will you commit to doing as a result of this exercise?

_____
_____

By when will you do it?

_____
_____

No Doubt Notebook

Our brain works in patterns. These patterns can be strong enough to get in our way. If, over the years, you have been skeptical or have mistrusted your intuition, then your brain will work hard to keep that pattern. Think of it as a mental habit of mistrust.

It is possible to have an amazing intuitive moment, one that eliminates all your doubt. And then, a few days later, you are back to disbelieving. This is because the mind naturally falls back to its old framework.

If you are opening up or honing your intuition, self-doubt can get in the way and block your abilities. The No Doubt Notebook is your friend, your partner helping you reprogram your mental patterns.

When you have an amazing intuitive experience, write it down in your No Doubt Notebook. In the future, when you find yourself doubting if this 'intuition thing' is even real, flip open your No Doubt Notebook and read through your past accomplishments. Your brain will correct the patterns and retrain itself to let go of self-doubt.

In time, you will no longer need this notebook. But for now, use it as a tool to keep yourself walking down the path you desire.

No Doubt Notebook

Strong Intuitive Experiences

No Doubt Notebook

Strong Intuitive Experiences

Session 1 — Reclaiming Your Focus

No Doubt Notebook

Strong Intuitive Experiences

No Doubt Notebook

Strong Intuitive Experiences

Session 1 — Reclaiming Your Focus

No Doubt Notebook

Strong Intuitive Experiences

No Doubt Notebook

Strong Intuitive Experiences

Session 1 — Reclaiming Your Focus

No Doubt Notebook

Strong Intuitive Experiences

Five-Minute Faith Practice

My Faith Speech:
_____
_____
_____
_____
_____
_____
_____
_____

Everyday, for the next seven days, read your faith speech out loud or to yourself. Allow yourself five full minutes of belief and faith. Record below any awareness or events that happened as a result of your faith practice.

Day 1: _____

Day 2: _____

Day 3: _____

Day 4: _____

Day 5: _____

Day 6: _____

Day 7: _____

Nightly Evaluation Sheet

Think of a brick wall, a problem in your life right now. Have you taken steps to solve the problem or have you remained stuck?

_____
_____

What would you like to do tomorrow to back away from the brick wall and move toward a solution?

_____
_____

Was there an event you responded to instead of reacted to today?

_____
_____

If yes, what specifically did you do?

_____
_____

Was there an event you reacted to instead of responded to today?

_____
_____

If yes, what was the energetic result of your reaction?

_____
_____

Is there anything you would like to do differently tomorrow?

_____
_____

Nightly Evaluation Sheet

Think of a brick wall, a problem in your life right now. Have you taken steps to solve the problem or have you remained stuck?
_____
_____

What would you like to do tomorrow to back away from the brick wall and move toward a solution?
_____
_____

Was there an event you responded to instead of reacted to today?
_____
_____

If yes, what specifically did you do?
_____
_____

Was there an event you reacted to instead of responded to today?
_____
_____

If yes, what was the energetic result of your reaction?
_____
_____

Is there anything you would like to do differently tomorrow?
_____
_____

Nightly Evaluation Sheet

Think of a brick wall, a problem in your life right now. Have you taken steps to solve the problem or have you remained stuck?

_____
_____

What would you like to do tomorrow to back away from the brick wall and move toward a solution?

_____
_____

Was there an event you responded to instead of reacted to today?

_____
_____

If yes, what specifically did you do?

_____
_____

Was there an event you reacted to instead of responded to today?

_____
_____

If yes, what was the energetic result of your reaction?

_____
_____

Is there anything you would like to do differently tomorrow?

_____
_____

Nightly Evaluation Sheet

Think of a brick wall, a problem in your life right now. Have you taken steps to solve the problem or have you remained stuck?

___
___

What would you like to do tomorrow to back away from the brick wall and move toward a solution?

___
___

Was there an event you responded to instead of reacted to today?

___
___

If yes, what specifically did you do?

___
___

Was there an event you reacted to instead of responded to today?

___
___

If yes, what was the energetic result of your reaction?

___
___

Is there anything you would like to do differently tomorrow?

___
___

Nightly Evaluation Sheet

Think of a brick wall, a problem in your life right now. Have you taken steps to solve the problem or have you remained stuck?

_____
_____

What would you like to do tomorrow to back away from the brick wall and move toward a solution?

_____
_____

Was there an event you responded to instead of reacted to today?

_____
_____

If yes, what specifically did you do?

_____
_____

Was there an event you reacted to instead of responded to today?

_____
_____

If yes, what was the energetic result of your reaction?

_____
_____

Is there anything you would like to do differently tomorrow?

_____
_____

Nightly Evaluation Sheet

Think of a brick wall, a problem in your life right now. Have you taken steps to solve the problem or have you remained stuck?
_____
_____

What would you like to do tomorrow to back away from the brick wall and move toward a solution?
_____
_____

Was there an event you responded to instead of reacted to today?
_____
_____

If yes, what specifically did you do?
_____
_____

Was there an event you reacted to instead of responded to today?
_____
_____

If yes, what was the energetic result of your reaction?
_____
_____

Is there anything you would like to do differently tomorrow?
_____
_____

Nightly Evaluation Sheet

Think of a brick wall, a problem in your life right now. Have you taken steps to solve the problem or have you remained stuck?

_____
_____

What would you like to do tomorrow to back away from the brick wall and move toward a solution?

_____
_____

Was there an event you responded to instead of reacted to today?

_____
_____

If yes, what specifically did you do?

_____
_____

Was there an event you reacted to instead of responded to today?

_____
_____

If yes, what was the energetic result of your reaction?

_____
_____

Is there anything you would like to do differently tomorrow?

_____
_____

Self-Evaluation

Are you where you want to be in your life? ☐ Yes   ☐ No

What would you like to eliminate from your life?
___

What is not in your life that you would like to add to your life?
___

How many minutes or hours do you find yourself smiling in a day?
___

How many minutes or hours do you find yourself laughing in a day?
___

How difficult would you say your life is right now? (Scale of 1-10 with 10 being most difficult)
___

What specific habits would you like to personally overcome?
___

What is one thing you could change about yourself that would make you proud of yourself?
___

What ideas do you have about why you were put on Earth?
___

Session 2

Core vs. Culture

One week in and you're already changing your path for the better! Now it's time to build upon your new foundation and expand your awareness. To be able to see intuitively begins with being able to see clearly our daily interactions. Clarity in life comes through curiosity, so let's get curious!

Topics Include:
Personal Programming
Our Spiritual Core
Breaking Through Assumptions
Releasing Old Belief Structures
Curiosity and Interpretation
Traditions and Ideals

Worksheets

Personal Programming

A Simple Review of Your Religious Experiences

Food for My Core

Food for My Core Checklist

Writing Your Eulogies

Assumptions, Interpretations and Taking Things Personally

Stay Curious

Nightly Evaluations

Homework Checklist

- [ ] Personal Programming
- [ ] A Simple Review of Your Religious Experiences
- [ ] Food for My Core
- [ ] Food for My Core Checklist
- [ ] Writing Your Eulogies
- [ ] Five Non-Cultural Moments
- [ ] Stay Curious Worksheet
- [ ] Suggested Book: *The Four Agreements*

Daily To-Do's for Students

Nightly Evaluations
☐ ☐ ☐ ☐ ☐ ☐ ☐

Food for My Core
☐ ☐ ☐ ☐ ☐ ☐ ☐

Stay Curious
☐ ☐ ☐ ☐ ☐ ☐ ☐

Personal Programming

In what region of the world were you raised as a child?
_____

Were you raised with any particular cultural base? If so, describe.
_____

What traditions were you raised with that you agree with?
_____
_____
_____

What traditions were you raised with that you do not agree with?
_____
_____
_____

What ideals were you raised with that you agree with?
_____
_____
_____

What ideals were you raised with that you do not agree with?
_____
_____
_____

How could your life have been different if you were raised in a foreign country, perhaps with a different family? What would have been expected of you? What would you have been limited by?
_____
_____
_____

Personal Programming continued

What is one food, hobby, or pastime you discovered later in life that you truly enjoy, something not introduced by your immediate family?

_____
_____
_____

Are there any traditions or ideals you resonate with that conflict with your childhood?

_____
_____
_____

Have you found a way to bring those traditions or ideals into your life while still maintaining balance between you and your family? If yes, describe. If no, what are some ways you can begin to find that harmony while still embracing that which resonates with you?

_____
_____
_____
_____
_____
_____
_____
_____
_____
_____
_____

A Simple Review of Your Religious Experiences

What religion were you raised in?
_____

What superstitions were you told about in connection to your religion?
_____

What spiritual punishments were explained to you (i.e. hell, karma)?
_____
_____

What spiritual rewards were explained to you (i.e. blessings, miracles)?
_____
_____

Were there any aspects of other religions you came across while growing up which resonated with you, or made you feel good? If so, what were they?
_____
_____

Are there aspects of other religions you have stumbled on, or searched out, that make sense or seem to "fit" with you?
_____
_____

Invent your own personal religion. What would it incorporate? Include beliefs, rituals, ceremonies, laws, sins, philosophies.
_____
_____
_____

Food for My Core

Cultural experiences that feed my core:
_____
_____
_____

Family relationships and experiences that feed my core:
_____
_____
_____

Social relationships and experiences that feed my core:
_____
_____
_____

Time management structures that feed my core:
_____
_____
_____

Physical sctivites that feed my core:
_____
_____
_____

Food for My Core continued

Personal rhythms and patterns that feed my core:
___
___
___

Personal living environments that feed my core:
___
___
___

Mental activities that feed my core:
___
___
___

Spiritual practices that feed my core:
___
___
___

Personal health choices that feed my core:
___
___
___

Food for My Core

Record each day what activity fed your core and how it affected you.
If you did not feed your core, how did that affect you?

Day 1
_____
_____

Day 2
_____
_____

Day 3
_____
_____

Day 4
_____
_____

Day 5
_____
_____

Day 6
_____
_____

Day 7
_____
_____

Writing Your Eulogies

Below, write the eulogy you believe would be read at your funeral if you had recently passed away.

_____
_____
_____
_____
_____
_____
_____
_____

Now imagine you have lived to the age of 100! Below, write the eulogy you hope will be read at your funeral.

_____
_____
_____
_____
_____
_____
_____
_____

Five Non-Cultural Moments

Over the next seven days, allow yourself five non-cultural moments that are distinctly spirit based and not based on cultural idealism. These may be moments that would surprise someone who witnessed them. They may be moments that create an amazingly deep connection within yourself spiritually. They may be moments that are considered "out there" in our current culture. Make sure these moments are true to your spiritual core and emotionally filling.

1
_____
_____
_____

2
_____
_____
_____

3
_____
_____
_____

4
_____
_____
_____

5
_____
_____
_____

Assumptions, Interpretations and Taking Things Personally

If a woman in a grocery store shoved past someone angrily, what might you assume? What is a completely different possibility that could be happening?

If you had to leave your home in a hurry one morning and were dressed in a crazy fashion, what assumptions do you think others might make of you? How do their assumptions affect your life as a whole?

If an authority figure or someone close to you takes a deep sigh and then walks away without speaking to you, what thoughts would you have if you took that personally? What thoughts would you have if you did not take it personally?

If someone in your life praised you for the work you've done, how might you let that define you? What if it was criticism instead of praise? Would you want to let that define you?

If you were to get a vision of a teddy bear with its head ripped off, what is one possible interpretation? What is a completely different possible interpretation?

If you were to get a vision of a man in a boat near lily pads, what is one possible interpretation? What is a completely different possible interpretation?

If you were to get a vision of four small children playing marbles in the sunshine, what is one possible interpretation? What is a completely different possible interpretation?

Stay Curious

Ask the question, "What do you mean by that?" five times and see where it takes you.

You follow your spiritual path. What do you mean by that?

_____
_____
_____

What do you mean by that?

_____
_____
_____

What do you mean by that?

_____
_____
_____

What do you mean by that?

_____
_____
_____

What do you mean by that?

_____
_____
_____

Nightly Evaluation Sheet

Did I experience any personal programming in myself today? If so, am I happy with my response to my personal programming? Does it fit my core?

_____
_____

Did I experience or participate in a non-cultural moment today? If so, how did this benefit me?

_____
_____

Did I find myself taking anything personally today? If so, how could I have changed my perspective?

_____
_____

Did I catch myself making assumptions today? If so, how could I have stayed curious instead of making an assumption?

_____
_____

Was there an event you reacted to instead of responded to today?

_____
_____

How much time did I spend today doing activities that feed my core?

_____
_____

What is one thing I can do to feed my core tomorrow?

_____

Nightly Evaluation Sheet

Did I experience any personal programming in myself today? If so, am I happy with my response to my personal programming? Does it fit my core?
_____
_____

Did I experience or participate in a non-cultural moment today? If so, how did this benefit me?
_____
_____

Did I find myself taking anything personally today? If so, how could I have changed my perspective?
_____
_____

Did I catch myself making assumptions today? If so, how could I have stayed curious instead of making an assumption?
_____
_____

Was there an event you reacted to instead of responded to today?
_____
_____

How much time did I spend today doing activities that feed my core?
_____
_____

What is one thing I can do to feed my core tomorrow?
_____

Nightly Evaluation Sheet

Did I experience any personal programming in myself today? If so, am I happy with my response to my personal programming? Does it fit my core?

_____

_____

Did I experience or participate in a non-cultural moment today? If so, how did this benefit me?

_____

_____

Did I find myself taking anything personally today? If so, how could I have changed my perspective?

_____

_____

Did I catch myself making assumptions today? If so, how could I have stayed curious instead of making an assumption?

_____

_____

Was there an event you reacted to instead of responded to today?

_____

_____

How much time did I spend today doing activities that feed my core?

_____

_____

What is one thing I can do to feed my core tomorrow?

_____

Nightly Evaluation Sheet

Did I experience any personal programming in myself today? If so, am I happy with my response to my personal programming? Does it fit my core?
_____
_____

Did I experience or participate in a non-cultural moment today? If so, how did this benefit me?
_____
_____

Did I find myself taking anything personally today? If so, how could I have changed my perspective?
_____
_____

Did I catch myself making assumptions today? If so, how could I have stayed curious instead of making an assumption?
_____
_____

Was there an event you reacted to instead of responded to today?
_____
_____

How much time did I spend today doing activities that feed my core?
_____
_____

What is one thing I can do to feed my core tomorrow?
_____

Nightly Evaluation Sheet

Did I experience any personal programming in myself today? If so, am I happy with my response to my personal programming? Does it fit my core?
_____
_____

Did I experience or participate in a non-cultural moment today? If so, how did this benefit me?
_____
_____

Did I find myself taking anything personally today? If so, how could I have changed my perspective?
_____
_____

Did I catch myself making assumptions today? If so, how could I have stayed curious instead of making an assumption?
_____
_____

Was there an event you reacted to instead of responded to today?
_____
_____

How much time did I spend today doing activities that feed my core?
_____
_____

What is one thing I can do to feed my core tomorrow?
_____

Nightly Evaluation Sheet

Did I experience any personal programming in myself today? If so, am I happy with my response to my personal programming? Does it fit my core?
_____
_____

Did I experience or participate in a non-cultural moment today? If so, how did this benefit me?
_____
_____

Did I find myself taking anything personally today? If so, how could I have changed my perspective?
_____
_____

Did I catch myself making assumptions today? If so, how could I have stayed curious instead of making an assumption?
_____
_____

Was there an event you reacted to instead of responded to today?
_____
_____

How much time did I spend today doing activities that feed my core?
_____
_____

What is one thing I can do to feed my core tomorrow?
_____

Nightly Evaluation Sheet

Did I experience any personal programming in myself today? If so, am I happy with my response to my personal programming? Does it fit my core?

_____
_____

Did I experience or participate in a non-cultural moment today? If so, how did this benefit me?

_____
_____

Did I find myself taking anything personally today? If so, how could I have changed my perspective?

_____
_____

Did I catch myself making assumptions today? If so, how could I have stayed curious instead of making an assumption?

_____
_____

Was there an event you reacted to instead of responded to today?

_____
_____

How much time did I spend today doing activities that feed my core?

_____
_____

What is one thing I can do to feed my core tomorrow?

_____

Session 2   Core vs. Culture

Session 3

Negativity and Perspective

A large universe will become very small this week when we bring it all back down to ourselves. Our thoughts create the universe around us and create the self. To find the origin of your intuition, you need to find the spiritual mind. We will detach, evaluate, and restructure our thought process to crack open to the spiritual mind and step into a fresh state of mind, a state of mind filled with endless possibilities!

Topics Include:
What Lies Behind Negativity
Shadow Work
Environmental Triggers
Automatic Thought Process

Worksheets

Rice Experiment Instructions
Rice Experiment Photos
Finding the Deeper Truth Behind Negativity
Shadow Work
My List of Negative, Self-Limiting Beliefs
My List of Positive, Empowering Beliefs
Five Minute Morning Gratitude
Positive Versus Negative Intuitive Exercise
Positive/Negative Exercise Results & Environmental Triggers
Five Minute Morning Gratitude
Nightly Evaluations

Homework Checklist

☐ Rice Experiment
☐ Shadow Work
☐ Finding the Deeper Truth Behind Negativity
☐ List of Negative, Self-Limiting Beliefs
☐ List of Positive, Empowering Beliefs

Daily To-Do's for Students

Nightly Evaluations
☐ ☐ ☐ ☐ ☐ ☐

Positive vs. Negative Intuitive Exercise
☐ ☐ ☐ ☐ ☐ ☐

Five-Minute Morning Gratitude
☐ ☐ ☐ ☐ ☐ ☐

My List of Positive, Empowering Beliefs
☐ ☐ ☐ ☐ ☐ ☐

The Rice Experiment

Masaru Emoto performed experiments with a high powered microscope to see the results of positive and negative forces on water. Samples of both clean and polluted water were exposed to words, sounds, and feelings that were either positive or negative. The results were visually stunning. Because we do not have a high powered microscope and time in the lab to recreate this experiment, you will be experimenting with rice right in the comfort of your home. If you would like more information on Masaru Emoto you can read his book *The Hidden Messages in Water* and/or watch the corresponding documentary.

Experiment Instructions:

1. Cook a batch of white rice in water. Any type of white rice will work. Do not add salt or flavorings.

2. Use two sterile and similar jars, placing a portion of the cooked rice in each.

3. Seal both jars tight with a lid.

4. On one jar write negative statements. This is your negative jar. On the other jar write positive statements. This is your positive jar.

5. Place the jars approximately 6-12 inches away from each other. They should be placed in the same temperature and sunlight conditions.

6. Once a day, twice if possible, hold each rice container (one at a time) and project your thoughts into the rice. First, pick up the negative jar. Think negative thoughts, focus negative energy going into the rice and speak negative statements to the rice, hate the rice. Set the negative jar down. Next, pick up the positive jar. Think positive thoughts, focus positive energy going into the rice and speak positive statements to it, love the rice. Set the positive jar down.

After 30 days, witness what the power of your thoughts and words can create!

Emoto's Water Molecules

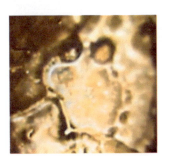

Before Offering a Prayer

After Offering a Prayer

"Thank You"

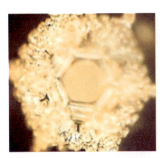

Love and Appreciation

"You make me sick," "I will kill you."

Photos of a Rice Experiment

Session 3   Negativity and Perspective

Finding the Deeper Truth Behind Negative Judgements and Thoughts

Negative thoughts and judgements are always surface experiences of a deeper desire or belief. Use this exercise to see if you can get to the bottom of what it is you stand for and believe in.

Negative Thought or Judgement No. 1
___

What fear or discomfort does the thought come from?
___

What would you like to see happen to ease the fear or discomfort?
___

What is the actual truth behind the thought?
___

Negative Thought or Judgement No. 2
___

What fear or discomfort does the thought come from?
___

What would you like to see happen to ease the fear or discomfort?
___

What is the actual truth behind the thought?
___

Negative Thought or Judgement No. 3
___

What fear or discomfort does the thought come from?
___

What would you like to see happen to ease the fear or discomfort?
___

What is the actual truth behind the thought?
___

Shadow Work

Some Truths about Shadow Work

- When we are angry at someone else, we are truly angry with ourselves.
- Our personal relationships provide us with opportunities to improve ourselves.
- Anger and frustration is a spiritual signal to take a look at ourselves.
- Other people's behavior can spark triggers within ourselves.
- Shadow Work is a gift, a mirror to use on ourselves.

Notice how each of those sentences end in "ourselves." This is because Shadow Work is about you and only you. Let your frustration and anger be a signal to shift from blame to awareness to opportunity.

Shadow Work Worksheet

Think of a situation where you were angered by another individual. What did they do that angered you?

_____

_____

Now disconnect yourself from the anger and step out of the experience. Review the situation again from an outside perspective. What are some possible reasons, not personal to yourself, as to why this person behaved the way they did?

_____

_____

Without anger, what are some possibilities involving the entire situation you may not have initially thought of?

_____

_____

Now, seeing it without anger and from a perspective of understanding, where did your original anger truly come from? What personal trigger of yours was sparked by the situation?

_____

_____

Examine your personal trigger and what role it plays in your life. What experiences in your life set up this personal trigger for you?

_____

_____

What can you do to take steps toward releasing the trigger or what can you do to remove the trigger all together?

_____

_____

My List of Negative, Self-Limiting Beliefs

Sit quietly somewhere and let loose! Create a list of twenty negative, non-flattering, limiting, or discouraging thoughts you have about yourself. When you're done, burn it. As it transforms into smoke, imagine your higher self taking the statements and releasing them from you, and you never having to worry about them again! Please burn safely.

You must fill up all twenty spaces. You may also add more if needed. Make sure you always burn in a safe container and environment.

Examples of negative, self-limiting beliefs — I can't lose weight. My hair is ugly. I'll never be successful. I'm not good enough. I'll never have enough money. People don't like me. I have a bad temper.

1. _____
2. _____
3. _____
4. _____
5. _____
6. _____
7. _____
8. _____
9. _____
10. _____
11. _____
12. _____
13. _____
14. _____
15. _____
16. _____
17. _____
18. _____
19. _____
20. _____

My List of Positive, Empowering Beliefs

It is important to complete this list **only** after you have completed the *My List of Negative, Self Limiting Beliefs* worksheet. It is important to release the old before building up the new.

We tend to easily list the negatives while it can be hard to list the positives. But please be egotistical on this sheet! You are wonderful and it is time to finally state that fact!

After completing this sheet, put it into your pocket everyday and read it to yourself at least once a day. Reading it silently to yourself is okay. Reading it out loud is better. Reading it out loud to yourself in a mirror is gold! Things that are wonderful about me...

1. _____
2. _____
3. _____
4. _____
5. _____
6. _____
7. _____
8. _____
9. _____
10. _____
11. _____
12. _____
13. _____
14. _____
15. _____
16. _____
17. _____
18. _____
19. _____
20. _____

Five-Minute Morning Gratitude

Everyday, for the next seven days, spend five minutes each morning bathed in gratitude. Explore the depths of your gratitude, the gifts you have received, and the experiences which have filled your life. Let yourself feel. Below, record a gratitude that deeply connects with your spiritual core.

I am grateful for _____. Thank you to the universe and the powers that be for sending me _____.

Day 1
_____
_____

Day 2
_____
_____

Day 3
_____
_____

Day 4
_____
_____

Day 5
_____
_____

Day 6
_____
_____

Day 7
_____
_____

Positive vs. Negative Intuitive Exercise

Using twenty index cards, write something positive on ten of the index cards and something negative on the other ten index cards. You should now have twenty index cards with positive or negative statements written on them. Fold all of the cards so they look the same. Fold them so you cannot see what is written on them and you cannot differentiate simply by looking at them. Put them in a bowl and mix them up. Select one folded card and, without opening the card, use your intuition to determine if the card is positive or negative. When you have made your intuitive decision, open the card and see if you were correct. It is helpful to keep a written record of your attempts.

At first it is best to simply hold the card and sit and wait to see what happens. Are you being pulled in a direction? Are you feeling cold or hot? Are you seeing images? Feeling emotions? Whatever comes to you is important to make note of.

More creative ideas you can try during this exercise:

- Take your time with each card, then try doing it fast.

- Try to picture the answer floating out in front of you, then try to picture the answer scrolling through your mind.

- Try to allow images to pop into your head, then try to do it with a blank mind.

- Sit quietly and see if you are pulled physically forward or backwards, then try to hold perfectly still.

- Try to sit with your emotions and see if they express what the card says.

- Go with your very first answer, then try going with your second answer.

- Label the physical space around you (left = negative and right = positive). Hold the card and step to the left, then step to the right. See if one feels stronger than the other.

By trying a variety of things, you will start to see where your abilities are the strongest. I wish I had a definite answer for you (step 1, 2, 3, etc.). But in the end, this exercise is going to teach you to listen to yourself **very** closely.

Also, make note of the moment where you start to get them right. Four in a row, five in a row, six in a row and then **WHAM** you get the next one wrong. It is in that very moment the most learning will occur. What did you do after the sixth guess to go from being "in the flow" to "out of the flow?"
This awareness holds the most important information for you. This exercise is a fine dance between going with the flow and analyzing which system works best for you.

Since it is only positive and negative, 50% is average. Anything above that and you might be on to something! Below you will find a score sheet. Do this exercise daily for two weeks. Each day, record your three best attempts. More importantly, record at the bottom of the worksheet any beneficial or hindering environmental triggers you discover while doing this exercise.

During each round of the exercise, intuitively read twenty cards. Record your three best results for each day.

Day 1: _____ _____ _____

Day 2: _____ _____ _____

Day 3: _____ _____ _____

Day 4: _____ _____ _____

Day 5: _____ _____ _____

Day 6: _____ _____ _____

Day 7: _____ _____ _____

Over the course of the next week, record below the environmental triggers you have found that benefit and hinder your results.

Benefits _____

Hinderances _____

Session 3 — Negativity and Perspective

Nightly Evaluation Sheet

Did you catch yourself having negative thoughts or judgements today? If yes, were you able to change these thoughts or judgements from negative to positive?

_____
_____

If you were able to change the thoughts, explain what happened as a result of changing them.

_____
_____

Did you have any opportunities to explore shadow work today? If yes, express how the shadow work enriched your life.

_____
_____

Explain what could have happened if you didn't do the shadow work.

_____
_____

What two positive, self-empowering beliefs do you truly feel confident about?

_____
_____

What is it you would like to improve on tomorrow?

_____
_____

Nightly Evaluation Sheet

Did you catch yourself having negative thoughts or judgements today? If yes, were you able to change these thoughts or judgements from negative to positive?
_____
_____

If you were able to change the thoughts, explain what happened as a result of changing them.
_____
_____

Did you have any opportunities to explore shadow work today? If yes, express how the shadow work enriched your life.
_____
_____

Explain what could have happened if you didn't do the shadow work.
_____
_____

What two positive, self-empowering beliefs do you truly feel confident about?
_____
_____

What is it you would like to improve on tomorrow?
_____
_____
_____

Session 3   Negativity and Perspective

Nightly Evaluation Sheet

Did you catch yourself having negative thoughts or judgements today? If yes, were you able to change these thoughts or judgements from negative to positive?

_____
_____

If you were able to change the thoughts, explain what happened as a result of changing them.

_____
_____

Did you have any opportunities to explore shadow work today? If yes, express how the shadow work enriched your life.

_____
_____

Explain what could have happened if you didn't do the shadow work.

_____
_____

What two positive, self-empowering beliefs do you truly feel confident about?

_____
_____

What is it you would like to improve on tomorrow?

_____
_____
_____

Nightly Evaluation Sheet

Did you catch yourself having negative thoughts or judgements today? If yes, were you able to change these thoughts or judgements from negative to positive?
_____
_____

If you were able to change the thoughts, explain what happened as a result of changing them.
_____
_____

Did you have any opportunities to explore shadow work today? If yes, express how the shadow work enriched your life.
_____
_____

Explain what could have happened if you didn't do the shadow work.
_____
_____

What two positive, self-empowering beliefs do you truly feel confident about?
_____
_____

What is it you would like to improve on tomorrow?
_____
_____
_____

Nightly Evaluation Sheet

Did you catch yourself having negative thoughts or judgements today? If yes, were you able to change these thoughts or judgements from negative to positive?

_____
_____

If you were able to change the thoughts, explain what happened as a result of changing them.

_____
_____

Did you have any opportunities to explore shadow work today? If yes, express how the shadow work enriched your life.

_____
_____

Explain what could have happened if you didn't do the shadow work.

_____
_____

What two positive, self-empowering beliefs do you truly feel confident about?

_____
_____

What is it you would like to improve on tomorrow?

_____
_____
_____

Nightly Evaluation Sheet

Did you catch yourself having negative thoughts or judgements today? If yes, were you able to change these thoughts or judgements from negative to positive?
_____
_____

If you were able to change the thoughts, explain what happened as a result of changing them.
_____
_____

Did you have any opportunities to explore shadow work today? If yes, express how the shadow work enriched your life.
_____
_____

Explain what could have happened if you didn't do the shadow work.
_____
_____

What two positive, self-empowering beliefs do you truly feel confident about?
_____
_____

What is it you would like to improve on tomorrow?
_____
_____
_____

Session 3 Negativity and Perspective

Nightly Evaluation Sheet

Did you catch yourself having negative thoughts or judgements today? If yes, were you able to change these thoughts or judgements from negative to positive?

_____
_____

If you were able to change the thoughts, explain what happened as a result of changing them.

_____
_____

Did you have any opportunities to explore shadow work today? If yes, express how the shadow work enriched your life.

_____
_____

Explain what could have happened if you didn't do the shadow work.

_____
_____

What two positive, self-empowering beliefs do you truly feel confident about?

_____
_____

What is it you would like to improve on tomorrow?

_____
_____
_____

Session 3   Negativity and Perspective

Session 4

Organization

Clutter in your mind and your energetic space create obstacle courses for your intuition. Life and intuition are always easier when there is a straight road to follow. At this point, it's time to pick up the speed and give your intuition the space it needs to flow. So let's restructure and clear the road!

Topics Include:
Organization
Decluttering Exterior and Interior
Streamlining Mental Pathways
Mind Mapping

Worksheets

Small Steps
Blank Schedule
My Life To-Do List
CHAOS - Can't Have Anyone Over Syndrome
De-Clutter Your Excuses
Mind Mapping Instructions
Mind Mapping Example
Mind Map To-Do List
Mind Map Overcoming Weaknesses
From Unmanageable to Manageable
My Life Purpose
Ten Things You Will See in a Day

Homework Checklist

- [ ] Small Steps
- [ ] Blank Schedule
- [ ] My Life To-Do List
- [ ] Declutter Your Excuses
- [ ] Mind Map
- [ ] Life Purpose

Daily To-Do's for Students

Blank Schedule
- [ ] - [ ] - [ ] - [ ] - [ ] - [ ] - [ ]

My Life To-Do List
- [ ] - [ ] - [ ] - [ ] - [ ] - [ ] - [ ]

Ten Things You Will See in a Day
- [ ] - [ ] - [ ] - [ ] - [ ] - [ ] - [ ]

Small Steps

If I were to make one small step toward my happiness I would:

_____
_____
_____
_____

If I were to make one small step toward my health and fitness I would:

_____
_____
_____
_____

If I were to make one small step toward my relationships I would:

_____
_____
_____
_____

If I were to make one small step toward my effectiveness at work I would:

_____
_____
_____
_____

Your Schedule

Time	Monday	Tuesday	Wednesday	Thursday	Friday	Saturday	Sunday
6:00AM							
6:30AM							
7:00AM							
7:30AM							
8:00AM							
8:30AM							
9:00AM							
9:30AM							
10:00AM							
10:30AM							
11:00AM							
11:30AM							
12:00PM							
12:30AM							
1:00PM							
1:30PM							
2:00PM							
2:30PM							
3:00PM							
3:30PM							
4:00PM							
4:30PM							
5:00PM							
5:30PM							
6:00PM							
6:30PM							
7:00PM							
7:30PM							
8:00PM							
8:30PM							
9:00PM							
9:30PM							
10:00PM							
10:30PM							
11:00PM							

Session 4 Organization

My Life To-Do List

Create a fully comprehensive list of unfinished items, clutter, and messes causing chaos in your life.

Below, list anything and everything you need to get done or you need to complete. Feel free to use additional paper if needed. When the list is finished, do not hesitate to ask friends and family to help you complete the tasks on the list! For seven days, spend fifteen minutes each day, and no longer, working on completing this list.

Examples... clean out the garage, update your software program, organize your photo albums, clean the fridge, call your cousin about the holidays, submit the tax forms, etc.

C. H. A. O. S. — Can't Have Anyone Over Syndrome

Create a place for incoming papers — Papers create quite the clutter. Over time piles can show up all over your home. Designate one location for all incoming paperwork and do not put papers anywhere but in that spot. When junk mail comes into the home, throw it away immediately.

Small Steps — Do not attempt to de-clutter your entire home in one day as it can be overwhelming. Begin with one room, one table, one drawer, one closet. When you feel how good the energy is in the newly de-cluttered space, you will be motivated to get up tomorrow and do a little more.

Create a "maybe" box — It can be hard to decide whether or not to de-clutter an item. If you are not completely sure, put the item in a "maybe" box and leave it there for a day or two. Come back to it later and see how you feel. If needed, use the de-clutter excuse worksheet on the next page.

Leftovers — What should you do with the left-overs, the stuff you want to get rid of? Put a load in your car and bring it to charity. Donate it to a good cause. Put it out on the sidewalk with a "free" sign (if your town allows) and watch someone in need come by and pick it right up. Sell it on eBay. Whatever it takes, just get it out of the house!

The Five-Minute Room Rescue — If you don't have a large chunk of time, take a five minute break or five minutes right when you get home to pick up and de-clutter what you can. A little goes a long way! Do this daily and watch your house progress.

One Year Rule — If you didn't use something for an entire year, like that specialty blender or the yarn you were going to knit with someday, get rid of it.

Do not leave a room empty-handed — If you want to make an impact over time, one of the easiest ways to do it is always leave a room with something in your hands. Get into the flow of always subtly de-cluttering.

No double-handling — De-clutter as you go. When the mail comes in, open it and deal with it immediately by reading it, tossing it, replying to it, or putting it in your "to pay" file. When you come home from shopping, take the tags off what you bought and put the items away. Double handling is leaving a pile to deal with later. Break that habit.

Do not be a storage locker for someone else — Sometimes friends, parents, or grown children will leave stuff at your house in storage — an old couch in the basement, yearbooks in a box, knickknacks they don't have room for. This stuff, which doesn't belong to you, adds to your energy field. Ask them to remove it or help them come up with a solution to get it out of your space.

De-clutter Your Excuses

What is your excuse for not de-cluttering an item? Every excuse has something important and meaningful behind it.

Challenge yourself to find out what is holding you back from the release. If it is impossible to totally de-clutter your item, find a middle ground.

My excuse for not getting rid of this item is:
_____
What feelings are connected to this excuse?
_____
What would happen if I didn't rely on this excuse and simply got rid of the item?
_____
If I can't let go of the item completely, what is one step I can take toward de-cluttering or organizing this item?
_____

My excuse for not getting rid of this item is:
_____
What feelings are connected to this excuse?
_____
What would happen if I didn't rely on this excuse and simply got rid of the item?
_____
If I can't let go of the item completely, what is one step I can take toward de-cluttering or organizing this item?
_____

My excuse for not getting rid of this item is:
_____

What feelings are connected to this excuse?
_____

What would happen if I didn't rely on this excuse and simply got rid of the item?
_____

If I can't let go of the item completely, what is one step I can take toward de-cluttering or organizing this item?
_____

My excuse for not getting rid of this item is:
_____

What feelings are connected to this excuse?
_____

What would happen if I didn't rely on this excuse and simply got rid of the item?
_____

If I can't let go of the item completely, what is one step I can take toward de-cluttering or organizing this item?
_____

My excuse for not getting rid of this item is:
_____

What feelings are connected to this excuse?
_____

What would happen if I didn't rely on this excuse and simply got rid of the item?
_____

If I can't let go of the item completely, what is one step I can take toward de-cluttering or organizing this item?
_____

Mind Mapping Instructions

Sometimes we do not move forward with big goals, events or tasks in our life because they can be too overwhelming. Creating a mind map breaks down something very large into something we can easily take on. By taking it out of your head and putting in on paper, you are able to see it from a new perspective!

1. Think of a large goal, event or task you would like to simplify. Write it in the center of a blank piece of paper and circle it. (e.g., 'My Balanced Life' or 'My New Business')
2. Next, draw lines radiating out from your goal to represent the major categories of your goal. These are the major areas you need to think about to organize your project and see to it that it can be achieved. Label the lines you create.
3. Expand on the major branches by attaching more branches to them. These exterior branches will either further explore the major category, or will end up being a to-do item or a weakness you need to overcome.
4. Continue branching off and labeling the branches until you have all of the exterior branches resulting in either to-do items or weaknesses.
5. Transfer all of your to-do items onto the To-Do List.
6. Transfer all the weaknesses onto the Overcoming Weaknesses List.
7. Complete the Overcoming Weaknesses List.
8. Transfer all your new found solutions for eliminating the weaknesses onto the To–Do List.
9. Your To-Do List should now have all of your to-do items and the solutions for your weaknesses.
10. Prioritize your list and number your to-do items according to what needs to get done first.
11. If any of your to-do items are too large to handle in one day, transfer them to the From Unmanageable to Manageable worksheet and break them down by months, weeks and days. Transfer these back onto the To-Do List.
12. Your end list should be a daily, prioritized to-do list. Now, simply start with the first item on the list and watch your large goal, event or task come to fruition.

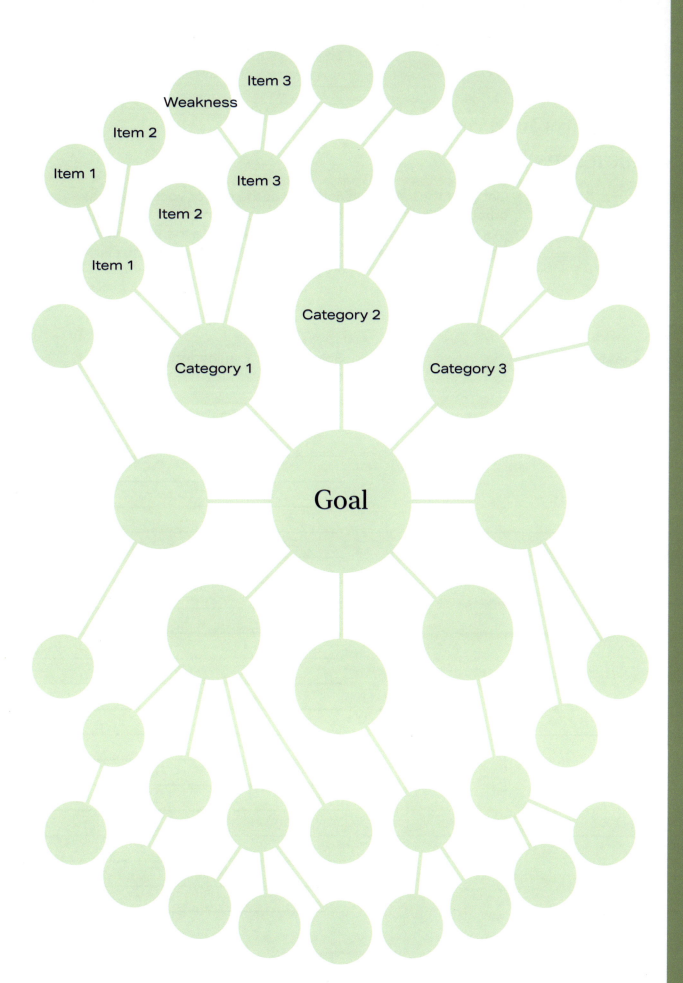

Mind Map Overcoming Weaknesses List

List all of the weaknesses found at the end of your mind map branches. Turn your weaknesses into to-do items! Write them on this list and brainstorm solutions to eliminate the weakness. Add your new found solutions to your Mind Map To-Do List.

Weaknesses	Solutions for Eliminating the Weakness
_____	_____
	_____
	_____
_____	_____
	_____
	_____
_____	_____
	_____
	_____
_____	_____
	_____
	_____
_____	_____
	_____
	_____

Mind Map To-Do List

Below, list all of the to-do items found at the end of your mind map branches and add any solutions you created from your overcoming weakness list.

You should now have all of your branches represented on this list. This will condense them into one easy-to-read list. Once your to-do list is complete, it's time to prioritize. Order the to-do items numerically according to what needs to get done first. When you are done, you will have a prioritized to-do list. Now, all you need to do is attend to the number one item on your list!

To-Do Items   Priority

_____   _____
_____   _____
_____   _____
_____   _____
_____   _____
_____   _____
_____   _____
_____   _____
_____   _____
_____   _____
_____   _____
_____   _____
_____   _____
_____   _____
_____   _____
_____   _____
_____   _____

From Unmanageable to Manageable

Do not let a large to-do item slow you down. Any to-do item that is too large to accomplish in a day can easily be broken down into smaller bites.

Large To-Do Item:
___

How many months do I need to complete it?
___

What can be done weekly to reach my monthly goal?
___

What can be done daily to reach my weekly goal?
___

My new Daily To-Do Item is:
___

Large To-Do Item:
___

How many months do I need to complete it?
___

What can be done weekly to reach my monthly goal?
___

What can be done daily to reach my weekly goal?
___

My new Daily To-Do Item is:
___

Large To-Do Item:
_____

How many months do I need to complete it?
_____

What can be done weekly to reach my monthly goal?
_____

What can be done daily to reach my weekly goal?
_____

My new Daily To-Do Item is:
_____

Large To-Do Item:
_____

How many months do I need to complete it?
_____

What can be done weekly to reach my monthly goal?
_____

What can be done daily to reach my weekly goal?
_____

My new Daily To-Do Item is:
_____

Large To-Do Item:
_____

How many months do I need to complete it?
_____

What can be done weekly to reach my monthly goal?
_____

What can be done daily to reach my weekly goal?
_____

My new Daily To-Do Item is:
_____

Life Purpose

Your life purpose will touch other people's lives just by doing it, no matter what it is. However, being true to who you are while you follow your life purpose will make the biggest impact on the world around you.

Also, it is limiting to believe you have only one life purpose. Feel free to complete this worksheet more than once if you have more than one passion.

Personality Traits
Aspects of ourselves that are organic to our spirit. They help make us who we are. Name two of your unique, positive, personality traits. (e.g., confident, humorous, witty, imaginative, loving, direct):
I am _____ and I am _____.

Character Traits
Based on beliefs. Name one strong positive character trait you have. (e.g., respect, devotion, honesty, organization, love, patience, compassion):
The character trait I hold most dear to my heart is
_____.

Passion
Ignites your emotions. What are you passionate about in this world? Name something you feel deeply connected to and energetically pulled to. What really pulls at your heartstrings? (e.g., children, the environment, religion, families, animals, government):
I am passionate about _____.

Drive
The pull you feel in regards to your passion. When considering your passion, what would you define as your drive for that passion? (e.g., to protect, heal, spread the word, bring together):
I am driven to _____ (my passion).

Now ltet's bring it all together

My life purpose is to be (personality traits)_____ and use my (character trait)_____ to (drive)_____ (passion)_____.

What makes you unique is what makes your passion powerful!

Ten Things You See in a Day

For the next week, take a few minutes out of each morning for this simple intuitive exercise. Sit down somewhere quiet. Ground, clear and protect yourself. Empty your mind. Ask your guides and/or the universe to show you what you will see today. Try not to predict through conscious thought what the answers may be. When pictures, words, or feelings come in, write them down on a piece of paper. They could be an umbrella, a bright orange car, a child laughing, a feeling of joy, a specific word, etc. Be open to anything and everything that comes through. Also, be open to how it comes through.

Keep the piece of paper with you throughout the day. When an item on your list appears in your life, check it off the list. At the end of the day, review your list of ten things and make note of how many you experienced or witnessed. Do this every day for two weeks. Take mental note of the days you checked off many of your items versus the days you checked off very few. What was happening for you on the good days? What was happening for you on the bad days? What environmental triggers may be hindering or helping you intuitively? If you were able to check off 4-5 items on your list in one day, you did very well. Write down why you believe you had either good results or less than good results.

Day 1

1. ☐ _____
2. ☐ _____
3. ☐ _____
4. ☐ _____
5. ☐ _____

6. ☐ _____
7. ☐ _____
8. ☐ _____
9. ☐ _____
10. ☐ _____

Total _____

Notes _____
_____

Day 2

1. ☐ _____
2. ☐ _____
3. ☐ _____
4. ☐ _____
5. ☐ _____

6. ☐ _____
7. ☐ _____
8. ☐ _____
9. ☐ _____
10. ☐ _____

Total _____

Notes _____
_____

Day 3

1. ☐ _____
2. ☐ _____
3. ☐ _____
4. ☐ _____
5. ☐ _____

6. ☐ _____
7. ☐ _____
8. ☐ _____
9. ☐ _____
10. ☐ _____

Total _____

Notes _____
_____

Day 4

1. ☐ _____
2. ☐ _____
3. ☐ _____
4. ☐ _____
5. ☐ _____

6. ☐ _____
7. ☐ _____
8. ☐ _____
9. ☐ _____
10. ☐ _____

Total _____

Notes _____
_____

Day 5

1. ☐ _____
2. ☐ _____
3. ☐ _____
4. ☐ _____
5. ☐ _____

6. ☐ _____
7. ☐ _____
8. ☐ _____
9. ☐ _____
10. ☐ _____

Total
_____

Notes
_____
_____

Day 6

1. ☐ _____
2. ☐ _____
3. ☐ _____
4. ☐ _____
5. ☐ _____

6. ☐ _____
7. ☐ _____
8. ☐ _____
9. ☐ _____
10. ☐ _____

Total
_____

Notes
_____
_____

Day 7

1. ☐ _____
2. ☐ _____
3. ☐ _____
4. ☐ _____
5. ☐ _____

6. ☐ _____
7. ☐ _____
8. ☐ _____
9. ☐ _____
10. ☐ _____

Total
_____

Notes
_____
_____

Day 8

1. ☐ _____
2. ☐ _____
3. ☐ _____
4. ☐ _____
5. ☐ _____

6. ☐ _____
7. ☐ _____
8. ☐ _____
9. ☐ _____
10. ☐ _____

Total
_____

Notes
_____
_____

Day 9

1. ☐ _____
2. ☐ _____
3. ☐ _____
4. ☐ _____
5. ☐ _____

6. ☐ _____
7. ☐ _____
8. ☐ _____
9. ☐ _____
10. ☐ _____

Total
_____

Notes
_____
_____

Day 10

1. ☐ _____
2. ☐ _____
3. ☐ _____
4. ☐ _____
5. ☐ _____

6. ☐ _____
7. ☐ _____
8. ☐ _____
9. ☐ _____
10. ☐ _____

Total
_____

Notes
_____
_____

Day 11

1. ☐ _____
2. ☐ _____
3. ☐ _____
4. ☐ _____
5. ☐ _____

6. ☐ _____
7. ☐ _____
8. ☐ _____
9. ☐ _____
10. ☐ _____

Total _____

Notes _____
_____

Day 12

1. ☐ _____
2. ☐ _____
3. ☐ _____
4. ☐ _____
5. ☐ _____

6. ☐ _____
7. ☐ _____
8. ☐ _____
9. ☐ _____
10. ☐ _____

Total _____

Notes _____
_____

Session 4 Organization

Day 13

1. ☐ _____
2. ☐ _____
3. ☐ _____
4. ☐ _____
5. ☐ _____

6. ☐ _____
7. ☐ _____
8. ☐ _____
9. ☐ _____
10. ☐ _____

Total _____

Notes _____
_____

Day 14

1. ☐ _____
2. ☐ _____
3. ☐ _____
4. ☐ _____
5. ☐ _____

6. ☐ _____
7. ☐ _____
8. ☐ _____
9. ☐ _____
10. ☐ _____

Total _____

Notes _____
_____

Ten Things You See in a Day Results

      Results   Environmental Triggers

1. _____ _____

2. _____ _____

3. _____ _____

4. _____ _____

5. _____ _____

6. _____ _____

7. _____ _____

8. _____ _____

9. _____ _____

10. _____ _____

11. _____ _____

12. _____ _____

13. _____ _____

14. _____ _____

"It is not the critic who counts; not the man who points out how the strong man stumbles, or where the doer of deeds could have done them better. The credit belongs to the man who is actually in the arena, whose face is marred by dust and sweat and blood; who strives valiantly; who errs, who comes short again and again, because there is no effort without error and shortcoming; but who does actually strive to do the deeds; who knows great enthusiasms, the great devotions; who spends himself in a worthy cause; who at the best knows in the end the triumph of high achievement, and who at the worst, if he fails, at least fails while daring greatly, so that his place shall never be with those cold and timid souls who neither know victory nor defeat."

Theodore Roosevelt

Session 4   Organization

Session 5

Guides & Manifesting

You are not meant to walk this world alone. Your connection to the divine is powerful and not elusive. Guides are beside you, working for your highest good. This week you will join their team and be an active part of your growth and learning. With commitment and determination, anything is possible!

Topics Include:
Spiritual Contracts
Guide Communication
Affirmations
Auras, Chakras, Meridians
Pendulum Work
Scrying

Worksheets

Guide
Commitment
Differentiating Between Guides
Contract Hints
Positive Affirmations
My Positive Affirmations
Auras / Chakras / Meridians
Pendulum Work
Scrying

Homework Checklist

- [ ] Differentiating Between Guides
- [ ] Contract Hints
- [ ] My Positive Affirmations
- [ ] Research Auras / Chakras / Meridians

Daily To-Do's for Students

Scrying Tool 1
- [ ] - [ ] - [ ] - [ ] - [ ] - [ ] - [ ]

Scrying Tool 2
- [ ] - [ ] - [ ] - [ ] - [ ] - [ ] - [ ]

Scrying Tool 3
- [ ] - [ ] - [ ] - [ ] - [ ] - [ ] - [ ]

Guide Commitment
- [ ] - [ ] - [ ] - [ ] - [ ] - [ ] - [ ]

My Positive Affirmations
- [ ] - [ ] - [ ] - [ ] - [ ] - [ ] - [ ]

Pendulum Work
- [ ] - [ ] - [ ] - [ ] - [ ] - [ ] - [ ]

Guide Commitment

For this commitment exercise, we will use a scrying technique. When we scry, we defocus. We let go of this reality and allow ourselves to be open to other realities, and in turn, to our guides.

For the next week, spend five minutes a day sitting in front of a light colored, blank wall. Sit approximately four to five feet away and stare at the empty space between you and wall. Let your vision fade away. Ask your guides to be there with you. Talk to them, about anything. Make this your personal diary time.

After a few minutes, ask your guides if there is anything they would like you to know. Then, sit quietly for a minute to see if you receive guidance. There are a few things you can do to experiment with this practice:

1. Sit with your eyes closed for a few seconds and then open them.
2. Light a candle and set it safely between you and the wall.
3. Designate a talisman for this purpose and use it only when communicating with your guides.
4. Play music. Select one song and play that song each time you do the exercise.
5. While staring toward the wall, feel the room. Are your guides behind you? Beside you?

Remember, this is about commitment. The guides will expect you to reach out to them every day. They are waiting to see if you are committed enough to "join" the team.

Differentiating Between Guides

For some, it can be difficult to differentiate between their guides. For others, they just want to get to know their guides better. This exercise is structured to help you distinguish the differences between your guides and learn more about them.

Set Up

- You will need two or more pieces of blank paper you can write on. Intuitively decide if you need two, three, four, etc.
- In a large room, place each of the papers in different corners of the room.

The Exercise

1. Stand in the middle of the room.
2. Ground, clear, and protect yourself.
3. Empty your mind and wait.
4. When you are drawn to one of the pieces of paper, walk over to it. Write on it any words, feelings, or pictures that come to you intuitively.
5. When you feel the intuitive information has slowed, put the piece of paper down and return to the middle of the room.
6. Repeat the exercise until you feel you are finished.

The end result will be multiple pieces of paper with intuitive information on each. Each of those papers represents one of your guides. This ceremony respectfully asks your guides to communicate with you individually and not as a group. It also provides you with more in-depth information about who your guides are and what their higher purpose is for guiding you.

Contract Hints

Your life contract was written by you. It is incredibly helpful when walking a spiritual path to know what you have expected of yourself. To begin to understand the essence of your contract, start looking at challenges in your life. We set challenges up for ourselves for a reason. Challenges are the cornerstones of your contract. When you improve yourself in this lifetime, you heighten the possibilities available to you.

Challenges in my life:

Name one personal challenge in your life right now involving relationships.
_____
What about yourself do you need to improve to ease or conquer this challenge?
_____
When you improve, how will this benefit your spiritual path?
_____

Name one personal challenge in your life right now involving only yourself.
_____
What about yourself do you need to improve to ease or conquer this challenge?
_____
When you improve, how will this benefit your spiritual path?
_____

Name one spiritual challenge in your life right now.
_____
What about yourself do you need to improve to ease or conquer this challenge?
_____
When you improve, how will this benefit your spiritual path?
_____

Positive Affirmations

Positive Affirmations build us up and make us strong. They rewire our brain and open us up to new possibilities. They empower us to take chances and to be our best. Making positive affirmations a daily practice strengthens your spiritual foundation.

Write it down	Writing positive affirmations on paper helps your mind to process them and it brings the affirmations into this reality.
Begin your affirmation with "I"	When you personalize your affirmations, the universe focuses its attention on you.
Make it short and sweet	Affirmations should not just be recited, they should also be felt. If affirmations are too long, you may find them cumbersome.
Do not use negatives...	Another way to say it is use positives! When you write your positive affirmations, make them positive! Refrain from using words like not, can't, won't, etc.
Be realistic	Impossible affirmations will not work. If you're short, you cannot become tall. But, you could lose weight or run a marathon.
Say your affirmation in the present tense	Keeping the statement in the present will give it more power. Avoid words like can, will, could or should in your statements. Say your affirmation as if it is happening right now.
Use visualization and emotion	Hold a clear vision of your affirmation. When you speak it, envision it and deeply feel what it is like as if it has already come true. Let yourself enjoy the end result.
Repeat them often	Repetition facilitates learning. The more often you say your positive affirmations the more they become a part of you and the more they will manifest.

Affirmation Examples

Book Recommendation:
You Can Heal Your Life by Louise Hay

I am open to the gifts of the universe.

I allow abundance to flow through me.

I easily let go of anxiety and stress.

I have an abundance of money.

I am good with names.

I am surrounded by abundance.

I feel joy each and every day.

I am fit, slim and trim. I only eat healthy foods.

I grow and learn every day.

I have peace of mind.

I am surrounded by loving, supportive people.

I breathe love and joy into my work.

I project good fortune to everyone I meet.

I release resistance.

I think positively about my physical body.

I control my thoughts and feelings.

I am in charge of my life.

I have a storehouse of positive energy.

My mind is sharp.

I run effortlessly.

My Positive Affirmations

Once a day for the next week, take a moment to say your affirmations.

Remember, affirmations are most powerful when spoken as if they have already happened or as if they already are. Feel it! Engage your emotions. Record any results below that became of your daily affirmations. Refer to "Positive Affirmations" in the reference sheets for instructions on writing positive affirmations.

1. _____
2. _____
3. _____
4. _____
5. _____

6. _____
7. _____
8. _____
9. _____
10. _____

As a result of doing daily affirmations, I:
_____
_____
_____
_____
_____
_____
_____
_____

Auras / Chakras / Meridians

Below are very basic descriptions of auras, chakras and meridians.
Pick one topic, and over the next week spend time researching it.
To select the topic, it is advisable to close your eyes and ask your guides to help you choose. Say the word "auras" and then wait. Say the word "chakras" and then wait. Finally, say the word "meridians" and wait. Decide which of the three resonates with you the most and dive into your research!

Auras — The concept of auras has been a part of many cultures throughout history. Auras are, in essence, energy fields surrounding all living things. For example, when an intuitive with the ability to see auras looks at another person, they are able to see colors and/or vibrations surrounding the person. Auras provide an intuitive with valuable information about an individual, an animal, plant, or even a piece of land.

Chakras — The Chakra system is said to have originated in India between 1500 and 500 BC. Chakras are an integral part of our energetic body, positioned at specific points within our physical body. Most cultures recognize seven distinct chakras, while some cultures recognize fifty or more chakras. Each chakra focuses on a specific aspect of a person's life. If a chakra is in balance, the corresponding area of the person's life is in balance. Practitioners evaluate chakras to determine how best to help their clients. Practitioners also balance chakras energetically.

Meridians — Traditional Chinese Medicine recognizes meridians as pathways through which life energy travels. One word for this life energy is "qi" pronounced "chee." These pathways have been mapped out on a person's body from head to toe. There are hundreds of points on the pathways which can be used to manipulate stuck qi and relieve symptoms the person may have.

Pendulum Work

Pendulum work can be done for a variety of reasons: to communicate with guides, to speak with spirits, and to ask questions of your higher self.

1. Find a quiet place where you will not be disturbed.
2. Ground, clear and protect yourself.
3. Hold the pendulum in your right hand, allowing it to hang approximately 6 inches below your hand.
4. Hold your right elbow tight to your side in order to reduce the amount of movement coming from your right hand and arm.
5. Hold your left palm approximately one inch under the bottom of the pendulum.
6. Swing the pendulum forward and backwards over the palm of your left hand, telling your guides this movement means "yes".
7. Swing the pendulum side to side over the palm of your left hand, telling the guides this movement means "no".
8. Now hold the pendulum as still as possible.
9. Ask if any of your guides would like to speak with you.
10. When the pendulum says yes, continue with yes and no questions until you feel you have the information you are looking for or the guides indicate the session is complete for now.

Scrying

Scrying is an intuitive activity found across many cultures and beliefs. The key to scrying is separating from the agreed upon reality and allowing your visual focus to fade. Sometimes it takes practice and a level of comfort with a new tool before we will see anything. Remember to keep in mind your environmental triggers when scrying.

Over the next week, scry with three different tools of your choice.

Scrying tools are any translucent, reflective or luminescent substance such as mirrors, stones, water, fire, glass, or smoke. For each scrying tool, do ten independent scrying sessions. Scry a minimum of five minutes per session. After completing ten sessions with your scrying tool, move on to another tool. Record below the tool you chose, which session you began to see results, and any intuitive information that came through during your sessions.

Scrying Tool No. 1 _____

Session with first results: _____

When you improve, how will this benefit your spiritual path?
_____
_____

Scrying Tool No. 2 _____

Session with first results: _____

When you improve, how will this benefit your spiritual path?
_____
_____

Scrying Tool No. 3 _____

Session with first results: _____

When you improve, how will this benefit your spiritual path?
_____
_____

Session 6

How Everything Works

After weeks of training, it is time to explore your new reality. To use intuition effectively, it is vital to understand where it comes from, how it connects, and the motivation behind messages. Deepen your understanding and expand your knowledge. Knowledge is power!

Topics Include:
Three Bodies
Crossing Over
Origins of Psychic Information
Origins of Mediumistic Information
Soul Connections
The Interconnected Web

Worksheets

Quick Kick-Start Exercises
Observational Awareness Exercise
Five Days and Five Senses Exercise
Card Readings
Intention Speech
Self Evaluation

Homework Checklist

☐ Self Evaluation
☐ Intention Speech
☐ Observational Awareness Exercise
☐ Suggested Movie:
   What the Bleep Do We Know?

Daily To-Do's for Students

Quick Kick-Start Exercises
■ ■ ■ ■ ■ ■ ■

Pick One Card
■ ■ ■ ■ ■ ■ ■

No Doubt Notebook
■ ■ ■ ■ ■ ■ ■

Five Days and Five Senses Exercise
■ ■ ■ ■ ■

Quick Kick-Start Exercises

White and Gray — Think of the positive energy in your body as white and the negative energy in your body as grey. Imagine standing on a platform of white light. Witness the platform rise up through your body. As it does, it pushes the grey, negative energy up. The grey, negative energy leaves your body through your third eye. Witness grey pouring out your third eye as the platform continues up your body. Eventually, as the platform reaches the top of your body, the grey will be gone and only white will be pouring through your third eye. When only white is remaining, your third eye is open and you are ready.

Brain Trees — Your brain is divided into right and left halves. Picture trees growing up toward the top of your head on both sides. The trees on the left side of your brain are swaying in the breeze from left to right. The trees on the right side of your brain are swaying in the breeze from front to back. Focus your attention on slowly getting the trees to all sway in the same direction. While you are doing this, your logical mind is distracted and your intuitive mind is free to speak.

White Room Meditation — To clear your head and give yourself the space to be in the moment, try the White Room Meditation from Discovery Meditation.

Grid Work — Set up a grid around you. Ask your guides to program the grid according to your highest good. If you are reading intuitively for someone else, ask for the grid to be set up according to their highest good.

Spheres of Light — Imagine hundreds of small spheres of light, approximately three inches in width, pouring through your head to clear your mind. The spheres enter through the back of your skull, move through the pineal gland and exit through your third eye. This action calms your logical mind and brings you into the moment. To move the spheres more effectively, and to be an active part of this exercise, imagine the spheres being projected faster through your breath.

Observational Awareness Exercise

Sitting inside your home, draw a picture of your front door as viewed from the outside. Do not look at the front door before starting this exercise. Draw the door the best you can including as many details from memory as possible. Once you feel you have completed it to the best of your ability, go to the door and compare your drawing to the actual door. Make note of the differences in your memory and the actual door. Now, sitting in front of the door, examine the door. Make a second drawing of the door, paying close attention to details and things you missed with the first drawing. When you are done, put the drawings away, out of site. Wait twenty-four hours. After twenty-four hours, without looking at either the previous drawings or the door itself, draw your door again. Compare this drawing to the very first drawing. Was there improvement?

Five Days and Five Senses Exercise

For five days you will focus your senses more acutely than you have in a long time! Spend your days consciously trying to utilize one particular sense as much as possible. For example, if you are focusing on taste, try tasting things you wouldn't normally taste. And, when you are tasting something new, focus only on the taste. Ignore your other senses, stop your conversations, close your eyes, embrace the taste. Same theory with the other four senses. Whether you are smelling, touching, hearing, tasting or seeing, focus on just the one sense. It is important to focus on sight the last day of this exercise, since visualization is our focus in this training. By the time you have completed the first four days, your ability to focus on your sight will be stronger.

For the first day, focus only on smell. Go about your normal day smelling more often than you are used to smelling. On day two, switch to touch and focus on touching as many things as possible for a day. Continue with hearing on day three. Tasting on day four. And finally, sight on day five.

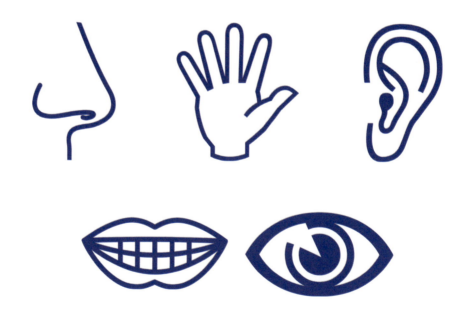

Card Readings

There are many different types of oracle cards. The key to card reading is to use a deck of cards that resonates with you. These cards are an extension of your intuition, so select them carefully. As a tool, cards give you a road map your intuition can use.

Examples of Oracle Cards

- Angel Cards
- Animal Cards
- Goddess Cards
- Wisdom Cards
- Healer Cards
- Spirit Cards
- Archangel Cards

Card Reading Rules

1. Do not use the book! Throw it away the very first day.
2. If you have time, sit with each card and meditate on it. Really get to know the vibration of each of the cards, as they are all very much individuals.
3. When reading for someone else, do something symbolic to infuse the cards with the person's energy. Perhaps, let the person shuffle the cards or cut the deck. Or ask the person to focus on a question while you shuffle the cards.
4. If, when shuffling, a card falls out and onto the table by accident, then you need to use that card in the reading. It was begging to be read!
5. Determine ahead of time if upside down cards make a difference in your readings.
6. After the first spread of cards, feel free to pick more cards as clarification cards.
7. Make sure to clear the cards of residual energy when you are done with the reading.

Pick One Card

Everyday, for the next week, do a one card reading on yourself. Ask a question about your life and then pick one card from your deck. That card will give you the answer you need. This will not only help you familiarize yourself with your deck, it will remind you to ask for guidance everyday.

Intention Speech

Before a focused intuitive session, it is best to use an intention speech to:
1. Remind yourself who your really are
2. Remind yourself why you are doing the work
3. Remind yourself to hold your spiritual space properly
4. Remind yourself to let go of the outside world

I am
_____

Sent here to
_____
_____

For the highest good of
_____

Please help me to
_____
_____

Now put it all together to create your intention speech.
_____
_____
_____
_____
_____
_____
_____
_____

Session 6 How Everything Works

Session 7

The Experiments

You've done the hard work and now it's time to have some fun!
In this session you will learn about two important tools for intuitive development and you will experiment to discover you own personal intuitive strength.

Worksheets

Self-Evaluation
My Dictionary Items
Psychic Experiment Notes
Mediumship Experiment Notes

Self-Evaluation

After weeks of applying new practices and concepts, it is time to review, reflect, and celebrate!

Name something negative you have eliminated from your life in the last few weeks.
___

Name something positive you have brought into your life in the last few weeks.
___

Name a specific habit you have personally overcome in the last few weeks.
___

Name something in the last few weeks you are proud of.
___

How many minutes or hours do you find yourself smiling in a day?
___

How many minutes or hours do you find yourself laughing in a day?
___

How difficult would you say your life is right now? Scale of 1 to 10 with 1 being the easiest and 10 being most difficult?
___

Notes
___
___
___
___
___

My Dictionary Items

Dictionary Item	Meaning

Notes for My Psychic Experiment

Notes for My Mediumship Experiment

What's Next?

You may have taken this course for personal reasons, to utilize your intuition in your daily life for guidance on your spiritual path. But, after completing this course, you may also be pulled to strengthen your intuition even further and help others on their paths as well. If so, the SAGE Method offers the Certified SAGE Practitioner Training program to support you in that journey.

If you wish to create an intuitive career that you love, or you are already established in that career, the SAGE Method provides the tools to help you strongly fine tune your intuition to amplify your professional journey.

The Certified SAGE Practitioner Training program is a perfect fit for people who would like to establish a strong career as an intuitive reader, life coach, death doula, energy healer, etc.

The program is built to assist you in improving your intuitive flow in connection to the work you are passionate about. It also supports you in building a thriving intuitive based business.

For more information visit https://thesagemethod.com

About the Author/Founder, Isabeau Maxwell

Isabeau "Beau" Maxwell is one of the leading spiritual coaches in intuitive development today. Isabeau brings deep channeled knowledge and personal understanding to the field of spirituality. She has helped people connect to their authentic, natural, intuitive abilities since 2007.

Isabeau is an internationally known medium, author, and teacher, touching the lives of people across the world. Known for her compassion and accuracy, Isabeau brings peace and comfort to many through her energy work, transformative sessions and teachings.

The founder of The SAGE Method, a life-changing, intuitive training program that teaches people how to open to their intuition and live an authentic, blissful life, Beau is also the creator of The SAGE Circle, Discovery Meditation and the author of *Cracking Open: Adventures of a Reluctant Medium*.

Having earned a bachelor's degree from Minnesota State University with a major in mathematics and a minor in chemistry, Isabeau maintains a balanced perspective between this world and the next. Down-to-earth and easy to relate to, Isabeau offers safe space for students and clients to process the intuitive information they are provided.

Made in the USA
Columbia, SC
04 February 2025